Gratitude

A Spiritual
Way of Life

Christine A. Adams

Copyright

Hanley-Adams Publishing

Boxboro, MA 01719

www.hanleyadamspublishing.com

Foreword

At certain moments, gratitude comes easily. We are full to the brim with joy, and that feeling naturally spills over into thankfulness for the goodness and grace of our lives.

At other times, gratitude is nearly unthinkable in times of pain and illness, loss and grief, trouble and worry. How can we be thankful at times like these? Why should we be?

Author Christine A. Adams maintains that it is at the times we're tried and tested that we most need gratitude. For gratitude revives our inner core. It reminds us of better times and the bigger picture.

Gratitude, as a way of life, allows us to draw from the bottomless well of the soul, to summon the peace and power, acceptance, hope and healing to get through to happiness.

In this little volume, you'll discover how and why to be grateful — always. You'll find techniques for realizing, renewing, and reflecting all the goodness in your life. You'll find how to "store up" gratitude, as a kind of savings account against the inevitable times of spiritual bankruptcy. We already possess all we need to be happy and at peace — the awareness of who we are and what we have been given. This is gratitude!

1.

Gratitude is an attitude of the heart. Thankful people live each moment with a sense of wonder and contentment. Count your blessings and watch them grow!

2.

Gratitude is like a magnet attracting greater happiness, a more fulfilling life, and more satisfying relationships. Every day let your heart fill with love. Gratitude creates more reasons to feel grateful.

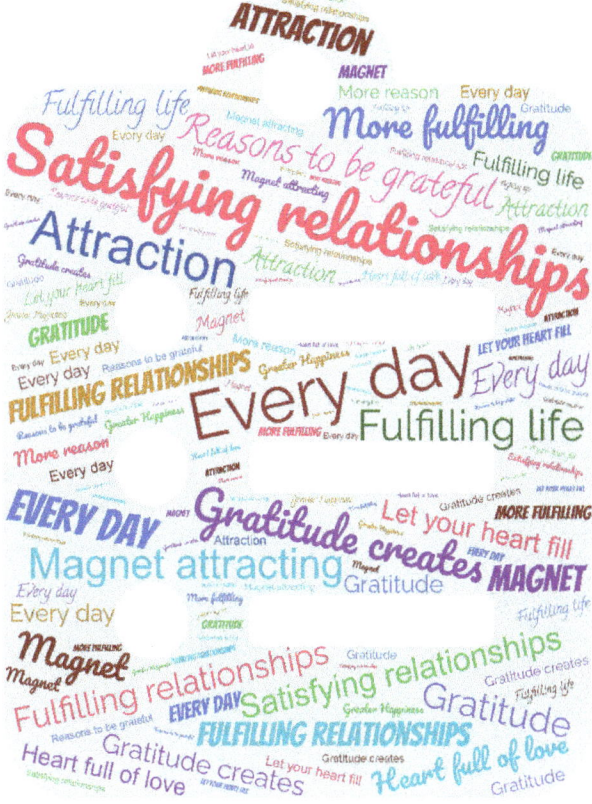

3.

Start a Love List. Beginning today, when you see, hear, or experience something that brings tears of gratitude to your eyes, write it down. Over time you will begin to see a pattern emerging. This will help to clarify what really moves you and to motivate you in living a life that matters.

4.

Each day is alive with new possibilities. Each moment is an extraordinary gift. You are right where you are supposed to be right now. This moment is all you have. Cherish it!

5.

When you wake up, listen to the birdsong. Greet the day with a happy heart, knowing that just as God provides for the birds, God provides abundantly for you.

6.

As you go through the day, be mindful of the little miracles that grace your path. Celebrate all the good around you and within you.

7.

Slow your pace...and open your senses to the world around you. Notice the vivid beauty of color — the brand new green of spring leaves, the fathomless red of a rose, the shimmering gold of a misty morning. Become the color you see. Look into nature's secrets to find yourself.

brand
green morning golden misty morning red rose
morningworld pace notice secrets fathomless moment morning
spring morning nature shimmering world shimmering
all your senses nature new
red colors shimmering nature
golden moment red rose beauty world slow all your senses
see slow look
world beauty leaves
vivid colors leaves
morning look notice
secrets red rose
vivid colors

8.

Listen to a butterfly flutter its wings. Stand near a waterfall and hear nature's applause. Throw your head back and let your soul rejoice to the song of the wind. Listen to the music of the universe.

9.

Hold still! Breathe in and out slowly, focusing on the life flowing through you. Let the silence hold you in its arms.

Be still and know God.

10.

Before you sleep, thank God for another day of life. Rest — knowing you are loved, you are blessed, you are held tenderly in the hands of a loving God.

11.

Watch the seasons change. All things in nature change, including you and your seasons of life. Embrace change! God is there in the barrenness, the new beginnings, the fruitfulness, and the changing colors of life.

12.

Eat slowly, with gratitude for the nourishment provided for you. Delight in deliciousness. Keep your body strong with healthy food and exercise, for your body is your instrument of praise to the Creator.

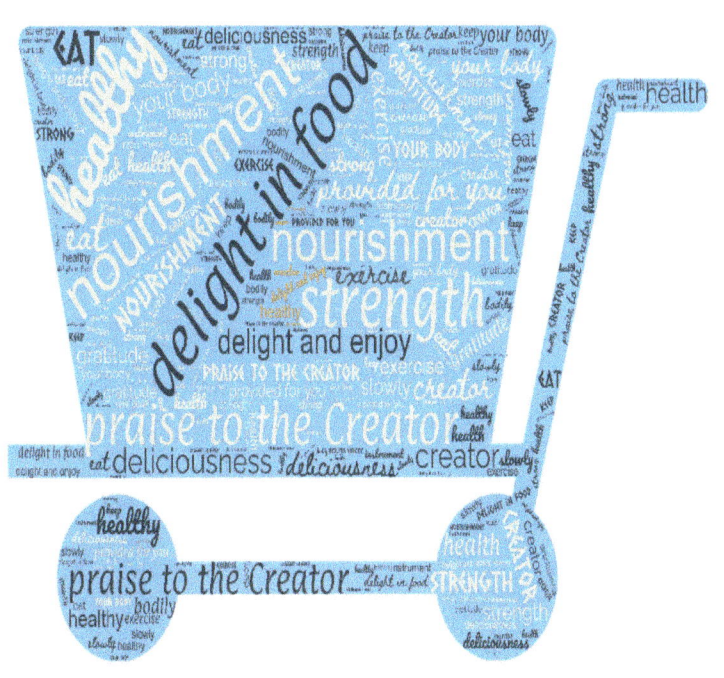

13.

What is your most cherished dream? Write it on a small slip of paper and carry it with you every day, as you visualize your dream coming true. Be thankful for who you are today and who you will be tomorrow.

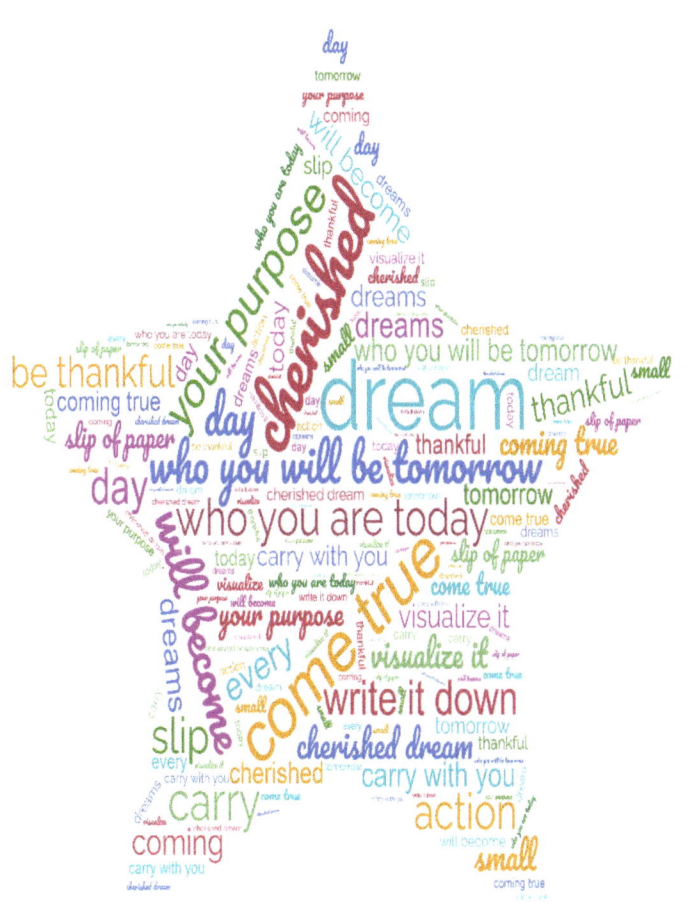

14.

Value every day by working at what you love. Don't wait until after you "get enough money" or when you "have the time" to do what you were made to do. Be grateful for your talents and choose to use them.

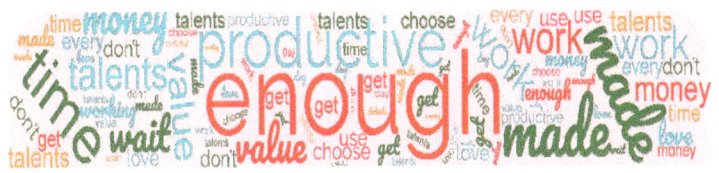

15.

Once you discover your life's mission, you are on your way to living the life you love. An inspired purpose produces courageous actions, which, in turn, create success. Commit to your calling with specific action goals.

16.

Grateful thoughts are healthy thoughts. They keep us focused on our dreams and steer us in the direction of personal achievement. Tomorrow is the result of what you do, think, and believe today. Believe that life is good, and it will be!

17.

When you reach an important goal, rejoice. Be thankful — for the confirmation of your dream, for your perseverance in making your dream come true. Hold onto the pure joy of that moment. Come back to it again and again.

18.

Acknowledge the people in your life: those you care about and those you dislike. Everyone you meet teaches you something. Be grateful for them and to them, because God is working <u>through</u> them.

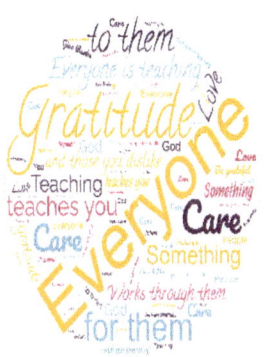

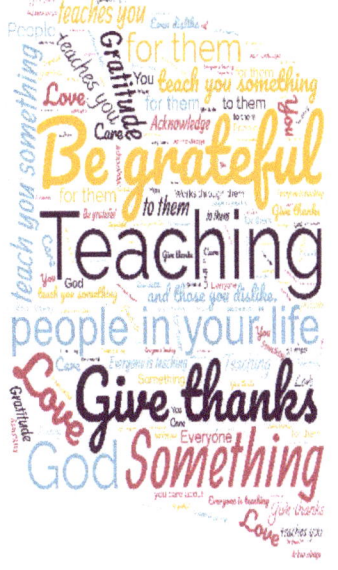

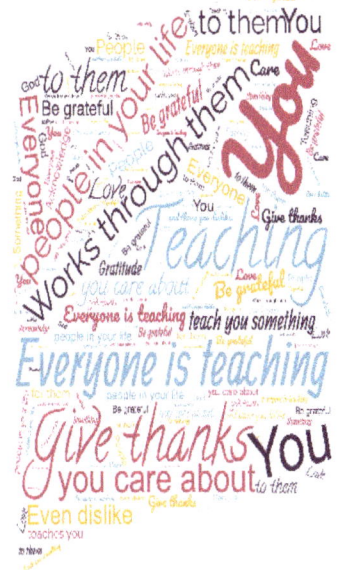

19.

Positive thoughts are healthy thoughts. Opening our hearts to the unconditional love of God is the essence of healing. Listen to your thoughts. If you think and say things like "This job is killing me," "I can't stand him," or "She makes me sick," your mind will believe you. Think positive; be well.

20.

God loves you as you are and is with you right now. Reassure yourself, "I am perfect in God's love." Speak "joy" to any negative, critical thoughts that crowd out gratitude.

21.

A sense of gratitude lets you know that you are a well-loved child of God. It empowers you to choose wisely — what you believe, how you feel, what you say, and what you do. Thank God!

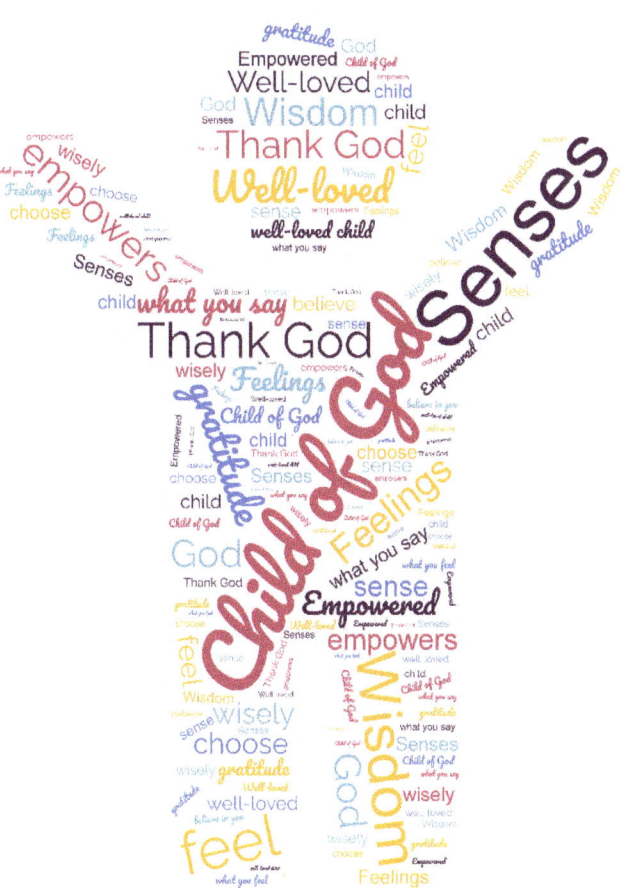

22.

You cannot be thankful and un-happy at the same time; it's emotionally impossible. God's will for you is joy. Accept joy, and realize that everything that happens to you — "good" and "bad" — blesses you.

23.

Be grateful for the journey of life, with all its twists and turns, detours and diversions. We often learn much more from the rocky road than from the smooth path.

24.

Be thankful, even in the face of adversity and distress. At times like this, gratitude means turning our will over to God's greater plan. Gratitude enhances the colorful canvas of our lives by allowing us to see the larger picture.

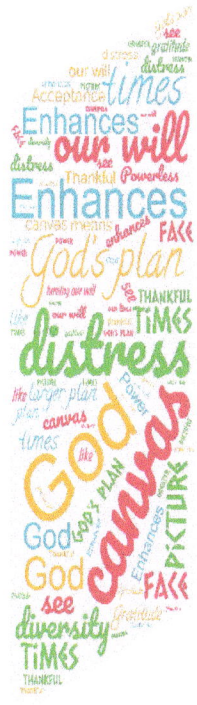

25.

A thankful heart redirects the mind away from fear and despair toward the love of God. Fear sees limits; gratitude sees possibilities. Fill your heart with so many grateful thoughts that no room remains for worry and fear.

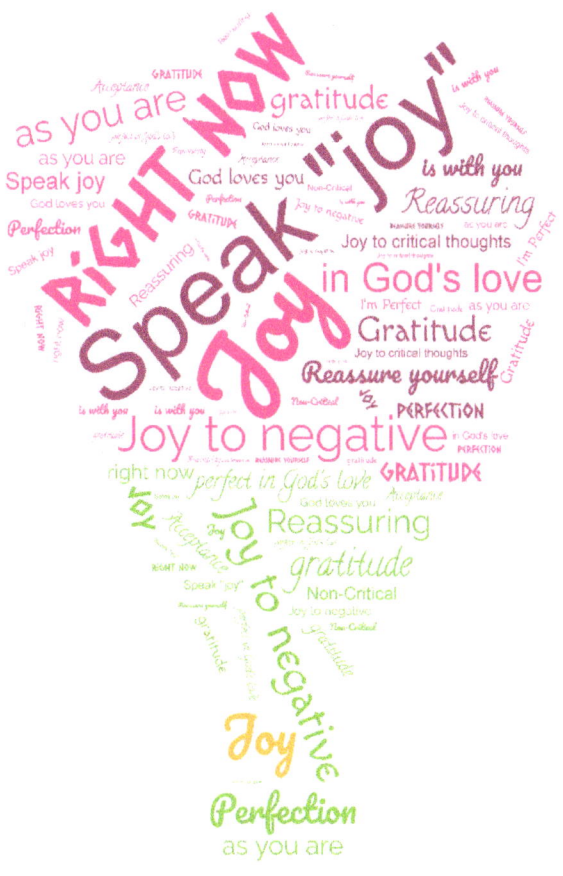

26.

As children, we may have learned to believe that we have all we need and deserve; or we may have learned to feel cheated, deficient, or helpless. Even if you have felt unblessed in the past, it's not too late to grow grateful.

27.

Gratitude has great restorative powers. When you're feeling down or unappreciated, make a list of all the wonderful things in your life. Write a thank you note to God.

Soon you'll be smiling.

28.

If regrets from the past crowd into the present, remember that there are no mistakes — just lessons to be learned. All things work together for good for those who love God and believe in Providence.

29.

Helping others benefits them, makes you appreciate your own gifts, and improves your mood. You can do volunteer work on a regular basis or simply spontaneously engage in acts of kindness. Help yourself by helping others!

30.

Ingratitude brings a sense of deprivation to our lives. Resentment and victimhood tend to repel others, so that we experience less love and support. Let go of bitterness; embrace thankfulness for what you have, who you are, and what you've done with what you were given.

31.

When your heart is broken, when a dream is shattered, when you lose something or someone important, it's hard to feel grateful. Remember times when you've felt the flow of grace in your life. Allow the gratitude from those times to wash over you now. Trust that God wants only good for you.

32.

Set aside some private moments for conversations with God. Ask for the inner wisdom to create solutions to any problems you face, and thank God for the help you know will come.

33.

Think of a situation that once appeared to be a problem but turned out to be a blessing in disguise. Think of a problem you are experiencing right now. List the ways you might ultimately benefit from this problem.

34.

Close your eyes and pretend you are watching your "life movie," beginning with the first day you remember. Bring the action up into the present day. Before opening your eyes, applaud yourself and the cast of people in your life.

35.

Tell those who help or serve you how appreciative you are. Tell salesclerks, waiters, postal workers, employees, friends, family, and perfect strangers. Share the gift of gratitude. Change the world!

36.

Say "Thank you!" — aloud, in a note, through a wave to a courteous motorist, via a gift. The person thanked will feel valued and appreciated. And when you make another person feel good, you feel good.

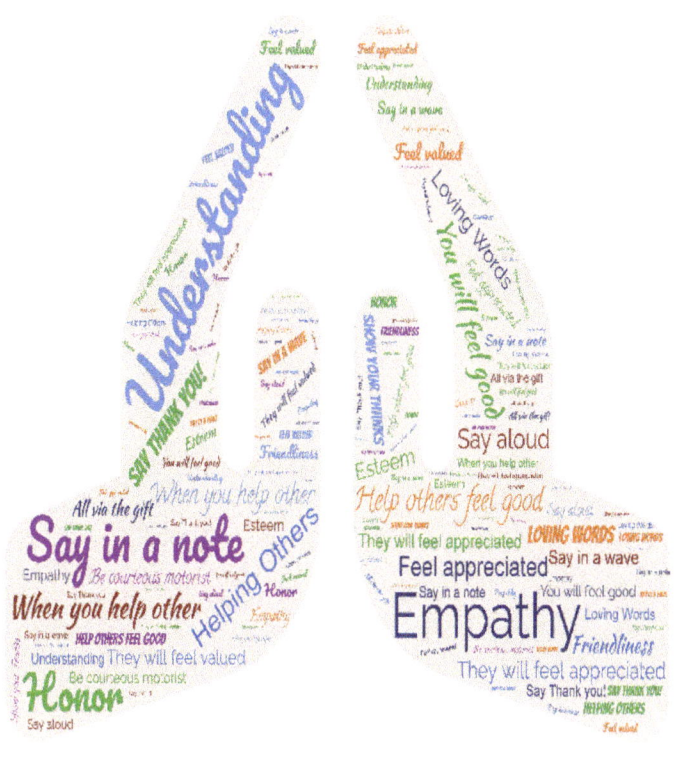

37.

The world needs you, and life is grateful for you. Honor your valuable contributions and talents, your productivity and energy, your words, and deeds. Take a moment to feel thankful for the self-worth you already possess.

38.

Put your faith in God's guidance, protection, and endless love. Together with God, you can do all things. Be grateful for God! Be grateful for God in you!

— *Notes* —

Notes

Notes

— Notes —

— *Notes* —

Also by Christine A. Adams

Seasons: Spiritual Meditations For
Winter, Spring, Summer, and Fall

Spirituality: A Life Force

ABC's of Grief – A Handbook for Survivors

Let Go and Let God

Teacher of God

Holy Relationships

Living in Love

September Love

Claiming Your Own Life

School Factory

Love, Infidelity, and Sexual Addiction

Gratitude Therapy

One Day At A Time

Learning To Be A Good Friend

Happy To Be Me

Worry, Worry, Go Away

God Made Us One By One

Watch for more at her website

http://www.christineaadams.com/

About the Author

Christine A. Adams, M.A., has been writing about issues of addiction, relationships, spirituality, and education for over 32 years. She has over 2,000,000 separate books and pamphlets in print with works published in 52 countries translated into 35 languages. Chris, an English teacher, was also formerly trained as an addiction counselor in 1986. However, most of her writing parallels her life experiences. Her early writings were about the alcoholic marriage, adult children of alcoholics, teen alcoholism, and sexual addiction. Then came books about spirituality, relationships, grief therapy and education.

In addition, she has produced 4 very popular Elf Help children's books: Happy To Be Me, Learning To Be A Good Friend, Worry, Worry, Go Away, and God Made

Us One By One. One of her best-known recovery books is the adult Elf Help gift book, One Day At A Time Therapy which is still selling in places like Taiwan, China, Portugal, the Netherlands, Austria, Sweden, Indonesia, and Brazil.

Her other books include: Spirituality: A Life Force, Seasons: Spiritual Meditations for Winter, Spring, Summer, and Fall, Let Go, Let God, Teacher of God, Holy Relationships, and ABC's of Grief: A Handbook For Survivors. Other books include a fictional narrative, based on her years of teaching, called The School Factory, and romantic novel, September Love. Visit her at www.christineaadams.com

Dedication

Robert J. Butch

To Robert J Butch, my late husband, who made "a way of life" living the concepts of this Gratitude book. Through sobriety and daily meditations, he always believed "Life is Good." Through two years of a debilitating terminal illness, he remained appreciative of life and love and actually lived with gratitude each day-"One Day At A Time". Today, I am thankful to have been beside him for nearly thirty years. Our loving memories inspire me and sustain me today!

John F. McKenna

To John F. McKenna, the McKenna family patriarch, whose diligence, generosity, and humility are legend. My brother, my friend, who over the years has gained the respect of family, business associates, and friends. He is a constant pillar of strength, much like the stone walls he has built in York, Maine. For his strength, wisdom and love, I am forever grateful.

www.ingramcontent.com/pod-product-compliance
Lightning Source LLC
Chambersburg PA
CBHW051546120626
46551CB00013B/1392